THE MOST INFLUENTIAL
WOMEN
IN BUSINESS

THE MOST INFLUENTIAL WOMEN IN BUSINESS

MARCIA AMIDON LÜSTED

Rosen
YA™
New York

Published in 2019 by The Rosen Publishing Group, Inc.
29 East 21st Street, New York, NY 10010

Library of Congress Cataloging-in-Publication Data

Names: Lüsted, Marcia Amidon, author.
Title: The most influential women in business / Marcia Amidon Lüsted.
Description: New York : Rosen Publishing, 2019. | Series: Breaking the glass ceiling : the most influential women | Includes bibliographical references and index. | Audience: Grades 7–12.
Identifiers: LCCN 2017056409 | ISBN 9781508179672 (library bound) | ISBN 9781508179825 (pbk.)
Subjects: LCSH: Women executives—Biography—Juvenile literature. | Businesswomen—Biography—Juvenile literature. | Success in business—Juvenile literature.
Classification: LCC HD6054.3 .L87 2019 | DDC 338.092/52—dc23
LC record available at https://lccn.loc.gov/2017056409

Manufactured in the United States of America

On the cover: Sheryl Sandberg was hired as Facebook's first chief operating officer (COO) in 2008. She speaks out about women working to close the "ambition gap" in the male-dominated business world.

CONTENTS

Today it's easy to think that women have always been able to attain high-status positions in the business world. Women who head large companies or start successful businesses are in the news every day. But it was not that long ago that business was a man's world, and only men could become presidents and CEOs (chief executive officers) of big corporations. Until the twentieth century, women in business were a novelty, and they often faced discrimination and tremendous challenges.

For one hundred years after the United States became a country, women struggled even to hold jobs. Society and culture dictated that women's place was in the home, raising children and keeping the house. Women were told that their proper role was to maintain a healthy and nurturing household, to support their husbands and sons in their important work in the world, and to train their daughters to be the next generation of nurturers. If women did have to work, those who had no husband or other means of support, the only acceptable professions were teaching and nursing, or domestic jobs, such as cooking, cleaning, or sewing. Nineteenth-century women had these areas of opportunity for working, but they were still limited by what society considered proper roles for them.

Women today are just as likely as men to hold high-level executive jobs with major companies or to start and run their own companies.

During the years between 1880 and 1920, women finally began to make progress in the business world, both as workers and as entrepreneurs. This was also the time when big business was becoming more important in the United States and helping the country achieve a strong economic standing with the rest of the world. More women began to work outside of their homes, but many of the jobs they held still fell under the category of being helpers or assistants. Women worked as secretaries and clerks in businesses, as salesgirls or supervisors in retail stores, or as laborers in factories. Some women were able to start their own businesses, but they still often fell into women's categories, such as clothing, cosmetics, and things for the home.

With the beginning of World War II, even more women entered the workplace. They were needed to perform work usually done by men, who were now fighting overseas. Even after the war ended, women continued to work and began holding managerial positions, even in large US corporations. The feminist movement of the 1970s inspired even more women to start their own businesses. By 1980, women owned half of all American businesses, and a decade later they earned one-third of all master's of business administration (MBA) degrees.

Today, women continue to start businesses and hold high-level positions in existing corporations. While there are still inequalities in promotion opportunities and pay rates between men and women, women are clearly achieving more and

more in the business world. From large corporations
to small companies, in technology, entertainment,
and retail, women are creating new businesses
and successfully running and improving on existing
ones. The women who came before today's female
executives helped pave the way for their success, and
the businesswomen of today will in turn open even
more doors for future women in business.

CHAPTER ONE

CLIMBING THE CORPORATE LADDERS

O f all the areas of business, large corporations have been among the most difficult for women to access, especially in roles beyond that of secretaries, administrative assistants, and other "helper" positions. And yet, women have found their places in the corporate world, sometimes by starting their own businesses as entrepreneurs.

"Cleanliness and Loveliness"

Sarah Breedlove, who would become famous as Madam C. J. Walker, was a woman of many firsts. She was one of the first female and African American entrepreneurs in the United States, and the first American women to become a self-made

Sarah Breedlove, better known as Madam C. J. Walker, shown in this 1914 photo, was America's first female self-made millionaire.

millionaire. She also pioneered a method of training saleswomen as beauticians to demonstrate her products around the country.

Walker turned a medical condition that she suffered from into a popular line of hair care and cosmetics specifically made for African American women. Walker was born on December 23, 1867, on a plantation in Louisiana. Her parents were recently freed slaves, and Walker herself was the first freeborn child in the family. As a child, she picked cotton and did household work and married at age fourteen. When her first husband died, she moved with her daughter to St. Louis, where her brothers lived, and worked as a laundress. She also attended night school and eventually met Charles Walker, whom she would marry. He worked in advertising and would later help her promote her products.

During the 1890s, Walker suffered from a scalp condition that caused severe hair loss. She began to experiment with home remedies to treat her condition, which led to her line of hair-care products that were made specifically for the needs of African American women. Her husband began helping her market her products and suggested that she use a more memorable name. Madam C. J. Walker was born. Walker began holding demonstrations of her products, and as they became popular, she opened a factory in Philadelphia, Pennsylvania. Here she trained women to act as salespeople, called Walker agents, by going around the country and holding demonstrations, promoting the products and Walker's philosophy of "cleanliness and loveliness." Walker organized conventions and clubs for her salespeople, a model that several modern cosmetic companies have followed. Walker was also known for her work for civil rights and for giving money to causes like education, the elderly, and civil rights groups. When Walker died in 1919, her company was worth more than a million dollars, and she left a legacy of philanthropy toward improving the lives of African Americans.

From Favela to CEO

Maria das Graças Silva Foster, while not from the United States, has a present-day story similar to Madam Walker's. She was born in 1953 in a favela, or slum, outside of Rio de Janeiro, Brazil. Her family lived in poverty, and Maria picked through trash to find recyclable materials to sell. But her mother was determined to see her daughter succeed and pushed her to get an education. Foster graduated from a nearby university with a degree in chemical engineering. She began working as an intern in production and exploration for Petrobras, Brazil's huge oil and gas company. Soon she was working for them full time. She was the first woman to actually visit one of Petrobras's offshore oil drilling platforms and help install equipment. Foster worked her way up the corporate ladder, earning a master's degrees in chemical engineering and economics and an advanced degree in nuclear physics. Her coworkers called her by two nicknames: "Graça" because she was friendly and likeable and "Caveirão" (a type of Brazilian armored vehicle used to stop riots in the slums) because she had such a strong work ethic.

Foster's abilities earned her a position as a government secretary for oil, natural gas, and renewable fuels for several years. But in 2005, she returned to Petrobras and became CEO of its petrochemical division, then of its distribution company. In 2007, the CEO of Petrobras, José Sergio Gabrielli de Azevedo, named her the first female head of Petrobras Gás. She also became a member of Petrobras's board of directors. In 2012, Foster became CEO of Petrobras itself. Foster feels an enormous responsibility to her company. "Power doesn't come by itself, it comes with responsibility and it's the responsibility I live with, which weighs on me, which wakes me up at two o'clock in the morning, takes me away from my friends, and makes me a more impatient and irritable person."

"All of Us Now Are Pioneers"

Like Maria Foster, Ursula Burns was born in an underprivileged area, a tenement section of New York City. And, in the footsteps of Madam Walker, she would become the first African American woman to run a *Fortune* 500 company. She was born on September 20, 1958, but even though her family was poor, her mother and her brothers and sisters encouraged and supported her. Talulah Smith, who interviewed Burns for CNN Money, wrote:

> Burns remembers people telling her when she was just a child that she had three strikes against her: She was poor, she was black and she was a woman. But she learned from her mother not to be afraid to ask for help or to accept support offered by friends and family members, people in the neighborhood, government organizations or nonprofits.

On the suggestion of her high school guidance counselor, Burns attended college and got a bachelor's degree in mechanical engineering and a master's degree a few years later.

Burns started to work for Xerox in 1980 as a summer intern and was hired when she graduated in 1981. Xerox manufactured printers, copiers, and other forms of document technology. Burns was often in the minority at Xerox, both as a woman and an African American, but she rose steadily in the company. In 2009, at the age of fifty, she became CEO of Xerox and helped make the company profitable again. By 2015, she had helped the company make $18 billion in revenue. She says,

> I say this to women all the time, particularly women trying to get into [science and technology], I guarantee [that] you will be the minority in the room. And instead of that being a burden, it should be an opportunity for you, to distinguish yourself. All of us now are pioneers. Every one of us.

Ursula Burns, president of Xerox Corp., is the first African American woman to run a *Fortune* 500 company.

Burns retired in 2017 as one of the most powerful women in the business world. She helped make Xerox known for more than making paper photocopies. She is currently focused on working as a mentor and helping others to get ahead. "Find one person you can mentor and help, and carry him or her along with you," she says.

On a Mission

Another woman who was a pioneer as the first female head of an international company is Virginia "Ginni" Rometty. Since 2012, she has been the chairman, president, and CEO of IBM (International Business Machines), a company known for first marketing business machines and then software and computers. Rometty was born on July 29, 1957, in Chicago, Illinois. She earned a bachelor's degree in computer science and electrical engineering at a time when very few women studied STEM (science, technology, engineering, and mathematics) subjects. She began working for IBM in 1981 as a systems engineer.

Rometty worked for a senior executive at IBM, and when he decided to leave IBM for another job, he felt that Rometty was the best candidate to replace him. But when she was offered the job, she wasn't sure if she should take it:

I said, tsk, it's too early. I'm not ready. Just

Ginni Rometty, the first female head of IBM, has led the company in technological transformation rather than sticking to outdated planning.

give me a few more years and I'd be ready for this. I need to go home and I need to go sleep on that. [My husband] sat and listened patiently to my story ... then he looked at me and he said, do you think a man would have

INVENTED IT

The company IBM has been in existence since 1911. It can claim to have invented many important pieces of technology, including the automatic teller machine (ATM), floppy disks, hard drives, laser supermarket scanning stations that read product information, magnetic strips (found on credit and bank cards), the UPC bar code, and the SQL programming language. In 1981, IBM premiered one of its most important products: the personal computer, or PC, which was intended to be used in homes, schools, and small businesses. The IBM PC was part of the new era of computers, when they became smaller and more affordable. IBM still holds more patents than any other company.

answered the question that way? And I went in the next day and I took that job.

Since becoming the first female head of IBM, Rometty has sold off parts of IBM that were not profitable and worked to develop new technologies, such as data-analysis software, cloud computing, and the Watson artificial intelligence technology, used to analyze data for hospitals, universities, and businesses. She feels it is important not to protect

A NEW ERA FOR CARS

Automobile manufacturers are entering a new era of innovation when it comes to automobiles and how they are driven. One area that is growing in popularity is electric cars. These can either be hybrid vehicles that use both battery electrical power and a gasoline engine or totally electric cars that run on batteries alone and do not require any gasoline at all. Electric car owners simply charge their vehicles on a daily basis by plugging them into an outlet. Since about 2008, as gas prices have risen and concern for the environment and the use of fossil fuels has grown, the sales of electric cars have been increasing. However, the cost of electric cars can be out of reach of many people right now. Some states offer tax incentives to people who buy them, and manufacturers are trying to build and market less expensive options. Electric cars also require owners to be more thoughtful about their driving habits since most electric cars have a limited range of mileage on a single charge. Many cities are beginning to provide charging stations for electric cars, to give drivers more options. Car manufacturers are also experimenting with self-driving cars that don't require drivers, but they are struggling with drivers' reluctance to trust and feel comfortable in a car that they don't drive themselves.

the past planning of the company when what's needed is to transform it according to changes in technology. As a result of her efforts at IBM, she has become the eighth-highest-paid CEO in the United States.

Rometty has now worked for IBM for thirty-six years. Her rise through the company has had many challenges. As she told the graduating class of Northwestern University in 2017: "Growth and comfort never co-exist. I want you to close your eyes … and ask yourself, when have you learned the most? I guarantee it's when you felt at risk."

A Rule Breaker

One woman has not only become successful as a chairman and CEO of a major company but has also topped the Fortune magazine list of the most powerful women in business, as well as being the most highly paid woman who heads a *Fortune* 500 company. Her name is Mary Barra, and she heads the General Motors (GM) automobile company. Her success at GM comes partly from her willingness to break the old rules of manufacturing cars and to try new ideas.

Barra was born in Michigan on December 24, 1961. Her father worked for GM, and Barra herself worked on the factory floor when she was a student, as part of a cooperative program between her high school and GM. She received a bachelor's degree in electrical engineering and later an MBA. After college, Barra started at GM in different administrative and engineering jobs, then worked up to managing one of GM's plants. She became a vice president and then

General Motors chairman and CEO Mary Barra spoke during a session of the 2017 *Fortune* Most Powerful Women Summit, on October 10, 2017, in Washington, D.C.

was named CEO in 2014. She is the first woman to become CEO of a major automaker.

It has been Barra's willingness to break old traditions at GM that has helped the company come back from falling sales and safety recalls. She helped launch the Chevrolet Volt EV electric car and also bought the company Cruise Automation, which develops technology for driverless cars. GM has also started a new car-sharing service called Maven, to compete with Zipcar and car2go. All of these innovations have helped make GM's stock rise in value.

Barra also has loved cars ever since she was young and saw her cousin's vintage 1960s Camaro. She often takes GM cars in development out onto the test track to try them out. And yet she knows that the energy situation in the future will require different kinds of cars.

> We're going to have beautiful, innovative designs. We're going to put the right technology on the vehicle … the way the customer wants it. We're going to have the right quality and the right performance features. Repeating that process—it's as simple as that and as hard as that.

"Anything You Put Your Mind To"

Another woman who has succeeded in an industry that seemed to be oriented toward men is Marillyn Hewson, who is the president and CEO of Lockheed Martin, an American aerospace and defense company. Lockheed Martin is the biggest defense contractor in the world and supplies the US government with equipment such as ballistic missiles, combat aircraft, robotics systems, and spacecraft.

Hewson was born in Kansas in 1953, the daughter of a long-term civilian employee of the US Army. She earned degrees in business administration and economics and started working for Lockheed Martin in 1983 as a senior industrial engineer. She has worked her way up the corporate ladder in positions including executive vice president of several of its divisions. Hewson had worked in four of the company's five business units. She became president and CEO of the entire company in 2013.

Marillyn Hewson, president and CEO of Lockheed Martin, is another woman who has risen to the top of an industry previously dominated by men.

Hewson has helped Lockheed Martin move into producing more military hardware. She oversaw the purchase of the Sikorsky Aircraft Corporation in 2016, which allowed Lockheed Martin to build its own military helicopters. Hewson has been named to *Forbes* magazine's list of the "50 Most Powerful Women in Business" and "World's 100 Most Powerful Women."

Hewson credits her mother's example, particularly after the untimely death of Hewson's father, for making her into a strong business leader. "My mother, now 94, belongs to a generation of women who faced incredible adversity with quiet but steely determination. By refusing to let that adversity stop them from building a brighter future for their families and their communities, they paved the way for the women leaders of today. Just as my mother said, 'You can do anything if you put your mind to it, you work hard and you take that responsibility.'"

CHAPTER TWO

LEADING THE TECH EXPLOSION

W omen have also carved out a place for themselves in the technology industry. And while it may seem that the technology industry just started about twenty years or so ago, with the explosion of computers, the internet, and other digital devices, women began pioneering in technology as early as World War II.

Actress, Pinup Girl ... and Inventor

Hedy Lamarr, who was born in Vienna, Austria, on November 9, 1913, is usually remembered as a movie actor during the golden age of studios like MGM. She appeared in thirty-five movies, with

Though best known as a movie star of the 1930s through the 1950s, Hedy Lamarr was also an inventor and businesswoman.

actors such as Clark Gable and Spencer Tracy, and was known as one of the most beautiful and exotic actresses in Hollywood. She was also famous for inventing a type of radio signaling device. It was an important step in creating the technology for secure communication for the military and for cell phones, although this use for the invention wouldn't be recognized for many years.

Lamarr was also a businesswoman. In 1946, she and producer Jack Chertok formed a production company to produce the movie *The Strange Woman*. She was the only woman during this time, other than actress Bette Davis, to form her own company, and hers was the only one to succeed. Lamarr also worked with the famous millionaire Howard Hughes on refining his aerospace designs. Hughes called her a genius. She was known to work on the set of her movies then go back to her trailer and work on her inventions. Lamarr's entrepreneurial efforts make her seem like a woman of today who accidentally wandered into the past, according to Alexandra Dean, who produced a documentary on Lamarr. Unfortunately, she did not start to receive recognition for her nonacting work until 1997, by which time she had become a recluse.

More than "Pink and Fluffy"

In 1958, Janese Swanson was born in San Diego, California. Her father was killed during the Vietnam

War, and she was raised by her mother. From a very young age, Swanson was interested in technology, even though she grew up during a time when girls weren't supposed to be interested in things like science and engineering. She remembered being given a typewriter, which she quickly grew bored with until she took it apart and changed the keys so that she could type in her own secret code.

Swanson earned degrees in education and went to work in the software industry. She helped create educational computer games, including the software version of *Where in the World Is Carmen Sandiego?*, which was inspired by her work as a flight attendant. Then in 1995, Swanson started her company, Girl Tech, now owned by Mattel. She wanted to design and market technology products to girls, and part of her approach is to make electronic gadgets in colors like lime green and purple, instead of the usual "pink and fluffy" color schemes that so many manufacturers think they have to use for girls. At one time, Girl Tech also published a magazine known as *Girlzine*, as well as a line of books about technology and other subjects important to girls. The website, Girl Club Tech, had more than four hundred pages of features, including biographies of female role models, information about sports, science, and inventions, an advice column, and a special section to help foster good communication between boys and girls. Swanson also helps develop technology curricula for organizations like the Girl Scouts and the YWCA.

Swanson says that her mission is to change how society sees girls and how girls see themselves. She wanted to create toys and gadgets that weren't pink and have nothing to do with dolls, ponies, or princesses. "There is a real need in our culture," she says, "to introduce girls to technology-based products and electronics at an early age. It not only increases girls' self-esteem, but helps to broaden the opportunities available to them in the future."

A New Town Square

Angela Ahrendts is a woman who has risen to the top of a famous technology company: she is senior vice president of retail operations for Apple. This means that she oversees Apple's 478 retail stores, as well as its online sales. Ahrendts came to Apple from the Burberry clothing company, joining Apple in 2014. Ahrendts is the highest-ranking woman at Apple and the second in command. She has helped Apple redesign its retail stores and feels that these stores should become a new kind of community meeting place, or "town square." She says of Apple's stores, "In my mind, store leaders are the mayors of their community."

Ahrendts was born on June 12, 1960, in New Palestine, Indiana. She went to Ball State University and got a degree in merchandising and marketing and then moved to New York City to work in the fashion industry. She worked at three large fashion

Angela Ahrendts, the highest-ranking woman at Apple, oversees Apple's 478 retail stores around the world.

companies: Donna Karan, Henri Bendel, and Liz Claiborne. She started at Burberry in 2006 and helped them turn their reputation around and open new stores in new markets and create new clothing lines. Her move to Apple in 2013 would draw on her skills in updating brands and creating appealing retail store atmospheres.

WHAT SHE WORE

When Angela Ahrendts appeared on stage in September 2017 to unveil Apple's newest version of the iPhone, she was wearing a pink lace coat made by Burberry, a company she once worked for. In the days following the event, the media seemed to focus only on Ahrendts's coat, which cost almost $3,000, rather than why she was on stage and her important position with a giant tech company. One reader wrote to the website Tech Insider, "Why did a technology-focused site even publish something about her outfit? Your article is one that my daughter asks about, and requires a sit down with her and her two brothers to explain why it is of zero importance that this powerful woman wore a jacket and it was expensive." Many of the reactions pointed out that it was an example of how women are not taken seriously in the technology industry. However, others argued that her outfit showed competence and professionalism, whereas men in technology often appear in jeans and untucked shirts. Women have to work harder to present a good image.

Ahrendts's new version of the Apple stores includes changing the pace that customers experience as they move through the space, making it calmer and less frantic. Her redesign also showcases the artistic uses of Apple's machines and not just the technology itself. She also changed the Genius Bar feature—a tech support station that every store has, and which the former vice president called "the heart and soul of our stores"—into a "Genius Grove" located underneath real trees. She says, "I don't want to be sold to when I walk into a store. I want to be welcomed."

It IS Rocket Science

Some women are working in technology that actually is out of this world. Gwynne Shotwell is one of these women. She is

Space X CEO Gwynne Shotwell admits that her career began with a suit that she admired on a well-dressed female engineer.

president and CEO of Space X, a space transportation company that works with the government and commercial customers. But Shotwell admits that it all started with a suit. As a teenager, she had to attend a program on female engineers. Shotwell didn't want to be there and wasn't at all sure that she wanted to be an engineer, but she was interested in one female engineer, very well dressed in a beautiful suit, who spoke at the event. Shotwell remembers,

> I was fascinated with what she did but I also loved her suit. I went up to her after her panel discussion and talked with her about her suit and also what she did. I left that event thinking I could be a mechanical engineer. ... I don't know if I would have gone up to her if she had not been so sharply dressed. I was more comfortable talking to her about her suit than her career; that was part of my connection to her.

As a result, Shotwell did study mechanical engineering and went to work for the automaker Chrysler. She then worked for two companies in Los Angeles. Then she met Elon Musk, the entrepreneur, who is the founder of Space X and the cofounder of Tesla, Inc. He hired her as vice president of sales at Space X in 2002.

In her first year at Space X, Shotwell helped bring in $5 billion in revenue. Today Shotwell is president of Space X and manages all its day-to-day operations.

Forbes magazine listed her as among the one hundred most powerful women in the world. Shotwell also believes very strongly in promoting engineering careers among young women and that women need to be hired in all levels of companies. "There are women in key leadership positions, but we are missing women in important middle management roles. That is the test bed; that is where you create new leaders. In order to populate that, you need to have more women as new employees."

Ms. Fixit

Women have made great gains as executives in US businesses, but women in other countries have often had a much more difficult time achieving these kinds of roles. Aarthi Subramanian of India is an example of how slowly women have come to serve in executive roles in her country. In 2015, she became the first woman to serve as an executive director on the board of directors of Tata Consultancy Services (TCS), an information technology service company, and in July 2017 she became the chief digital officer there. Subramanian earned a computer science degree in India and a master's degree in engineering management from the University of Kansas in the United States. She started working with TCS twenty-six years ago, on projects in places like Sweden, the United States, and Canada as well as India.

A receptionist works beneath a portrait of Aarthi Subramanian, executive director of Tata Consultancy Services. Indian companies are now required to have at least one female director.

Subramanian's colleagues call her Ms. Fixit because they say she has a solution for any challenge that comes along. Subramanian says she has picked up many business and leadership qualities from her boss and mentor, N. Chandrasekaran. "The word 'rigour' is frequently used in TCS, and I really understood what that meant after working with him. It is all about being detail-oriented, looking at finer things. It's about perfection and not settling for the next best." Some of her projects, such as changing the process for Indians to get passports, are more difficult because of her culture and her gender, especially when employees resist change and want to do things as they have always been done. But Subramanian plans to continue devoting her energies to the company and her fellow employees. She sees herself five years from now with the same determination: Subramanian will never settle for anything but the very best. "I see pushing not just myself but the entire team to do new things and continuously pursue excellence. There should never be a dull moment."

A Great Comeback

Women in the business world have not been immune from the issues that can cause them to rise and then suddenly fall within their industry. But in the case of Amy Pascal, once a studio head at Sony Pictures, being fired actually led her to a comeback with a company of her own.

Pascal was born in 1959 in Los Angeles, California. She started her career in the entertainment industry by working as a secretary to a producer at a film company, but eventually she advanced to vice president of production at 20th Century Fox, then to Columbia Pictures, and finally to Sony Pictures Entertainment. She worked on movies like *Spider-Man* and the James Bond franchise, as well as television shows. However, when Sony Pictures suffered from a cyberattack in 2004, Pascal's private emails were exposed,

THE STATISTICS

India ranks the third lowest in the world for the number of women who hold executive positions in business. Women make up 24 percent of the entry-level jobs for management or directorships, but only 14 percent of executive officers are women. There is also a large gender gap in wages. Women in India earn 57 percent of what their male colleagues earn for performing the same work, according to catalyst.org. The more educated a woman is, the wider the gender pay gap, and that gap increases as women advance in their careers. However, the industries with the highest percentage of women on boards are technology, media, and telecommunications.

many of them not very complimentary about actors and political figures. Sony fired her in 2015, mostly because of her focus on movies made from books and starring major actors, instead of focusing on computer-generated special effects and franchises. It was a difficult situation for Pascal: "When you are the head of a studio, you are smart and fabulous and funny and good-looking. I didn't want to just be me again. The idea of that was kind of terrifying. That job was my identity."

Producer Amy Pascal attends the premiere of the movie *Molly's Game* in New York City in December 2017.

Pascal made a comeback, however, by starting her own production company, Pascal Pictures. She now makes movies for other studios, including the 2016 reboot of *Ghostbusters* and *Spider-Man: Homecoming*. She is also working on adapting other books into movies. Pascal says that her life is better now. "I will always carry what happened with me," she said. "There's no other way. But you scrape as much grace as you possibly can off the ground and you move forward."

CHAPTER THREE

RUNNING RETAIL

Retail jobs, such as working as a clerk in a store, were among the first to be accessible to women, and that tradition has continued. However, women have become the entrepreneurs who start retail businesses or the ones who take an existing company and make it bigger and better.

"Only a Woman Can Understand a Woman's Ills"

An early entrepreneur who transformed her home remedy into a successful business was Lydia Estes Pinkham, who was born in Massachusetts in 1818. Pinkham had created a home remedy made of herbs, which she made in her kitchen and shared with her family and friends. It was made from black cohosh, life root, unicorn root, pleurisy

Yours for Health
Lydia E. Pinkham

Lydia Pinkham's portrait on the labels of her bottles of vegetable remedy helped inspire trust with her female customers.

root, and fenugreek seed, all mixed with a large amount of alcohol and was said to be especially good at treating women's illnesses and symptoms. In 1875, Pinkham began selling her remedy to the public for $1 a bottle. Called Lydia E. Pinkham's Vegetable Compound, the bottle featured Pinkham's own portrait. Her son suggested that putting her picture on the bottle would inspire trust in female customers and lead people to see it as a quality homemade remedy. His idea proved to be very successful. Later ads referred to her as "the savior of her sex."

Even though it was never proven that Pinkham's compound actually cured any of the conditions she claimed it did, it was a huge success. Pinkham moved her production from her kitchen to a factory. She also began to publish informational pamphlets about different aspects of women's health and answer questions sent to her by women all over the country. Pinkham started a Department of Advice, staffed only by women, to answer these letters—as many as one hundred a day. Many of Pinkham's customers were afraid to discuss their problems with male doctors, and women's health did not receive a great deal of attention from the medical establishment. Pinkham's pamphlets, with titles like "Health Hints" and "Advice to Mothers," distributed sound medical advice. Through her compound company, Pinkham changed the lives of thousands of American women.

WHAT'S REALLY IN IT?

In 1906, the Pure Food and Drug Act was signed into law by US president Theodore Roosevelt. It was meant to prevent "the manufacture, sale, or transportation of adulterated or misbranded or poisonous or deleterious foods, drugs or medicines, and liquors." The act was partly in response to the horrible conditions found in food manufacturing plants around the country, some of which had been described in Upton Sinclair's book *The Jungle*, about the conditions in the Chicago meatpacking industry. However, the act also required patent medicine companies like Lydia Pinkham's to reveal exactly what was in their formulas. Many

(continued on the next page)

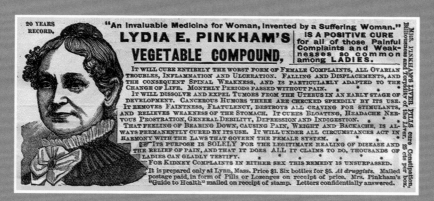

This advertisement for Lydia E. Pinkham's Vegetable Compound promised to cure a wide variety of illnesses and conditions, especially for women.

(continued from the previous page)

patent remedies contained high amounts of alcohol, as well as vegetable extracts and sugar. Some even contained things like caffeine, morphine, cocaine, or opium, before these substances were regulated. Pinkham's compound was shown to contain 20 percent alcohol (the equivalent of many liqueurs). As of 2004, the version now available, called Lydia Pinkham's Herbal Compound, still contains herbs and vegetable extracts like motherwort, gentian, Jamaican dogwood, pleurisy root, licorice, black cohosh, and dandelion, many of which are known natural remedies. However, it no longer contains the high level of alcohol.

A Homegrown Brand

Another modern-day female entrepreneur excelled at creating something that women wanted and needed. When Suzie Wokabi, at the age of thirty, returned to her native Kenya after living in the United States for ten years, she was shocked to find that the cosmetics she'd used in the United States were extremely expensive there. Worse yet, many foreign brands were not formulated for the skin of African women. Wokabi had worked in the American fashion and beauty industry as a makeup artist, and she saw that there was a need for a homegrown cosmetic line for African women. As a result, she started her company, SuzieBeauty.

"Put a dark-skinned woman and the African sun together, throw in some grossly overpriced, often counterfeit makeup brands into the equation and what do you get—a recipe for disaster!" Wokabi said. Her solution was a line of cosmetics that were high quality, yet affordable, and made specifically for African women, who have more sun exposure because of their climate. She also formulated the colors to work well with dark skin and its unique textures. After years of researching, developing, and testing, Wokabi launched her new line in 2012.

SuzieBeauty cosmetics have not only been popular in Africa, but all over the world. There are twenty-one SuzieBeauty retail stores, in addition to outlets that sell her products. The company also provides makeup services and trains makeup artists. In 2016, Wokabi sold her company so that she could bring in money to expand the brand. Wokabi is excited about the future of her company. "I never quite planned to be [a CEO]. My love is makeup artistry and because of my passion for beauty, I was led into this journey, which I now accept was always meant to be."

Just Doing It

Sometimes a retail cashier job can lead to much more, including management positions at what might

Ann-Marie Campbell began her career at Home Depot as a cashier, but with the encouragement of a mentor, eventually worked her way up to executive vice president.

seem like a man's business. Ann-Marie Campbell, who was born in Kingston, Jamaica, in 1965, started out working as a cashier at a Home Depot store in Florida in 1985. She attended Georgia State University, where she earned a bachelor's degree in philosophy and a master's degree in business administration. Campbell began working her way up in the company, as a store manager, district manager, and vice president. In 2016, she was named executive vice president for Home Depot's US stores.

Campbell admitted that she had never planned on a career at Home Depot, and she wasn't sure of her abilities until she found a mentor in a Home Depot vice president. That life-changing mentor asked her a question during a store inspection and her answer revealed to him her intelligence and potential.

"I thought I needed to be perfect. Women often think they have to know everything before they can step into a role. But my mentor told me, 'You can do this job.' He taught me to understand and own the value of what I brought to the table."

Crystal Hanlon also started working at Home Depot as a cashier in 1985, working at a store in Texas while she attended the University of Houston. Today, she is the president of the company's northern division. She also worked her way up through customer service to store manager to executive positions. Both Hanlon and Campbell were named to *Fortune* magazine's list of "Retail's 8 Most Powerful Women" in 2016.

Follow Your Heart

Some women find that even a successful career in medicine or law doesn't satisfy them. This is true of Jodie Fox, who founded the Shoes of Prey. Fox was a successful banking and finance lawyer in Australia. However, she decided she wanted more satisfaction from her work

Jodie Fox, founder of the custom shoe company Shoes of Prey, started her company because she was seeking more satisfaction from her work.

than she was getting. "I've almost always followed my heart. I've never made a decision purely based on money—Instead I am driven by the desire to live a full life of doing what moves me," she said. Fox started Shoes of Prey in 2009, creating a website where women can design their own custom shoes starting with about twenty basic styles as a blank slate. They can be designed in almost any size, color, or style, and customers receive them in about two weeks. Since Shoes of Prey started, customers have designed about six million pairs of shoes. They can "play" with their shoe designs on the website, rotating them for a complete view and zooming in on texture and design. There are also predesigned shoes for sale, and many of these are now sold in large department stores. Fox has proven that success can come not just from a high-level career, but also from doing what you really want to do and providing something that feeds other people's creativity as well. "People love what they create. That emotional connection cannot be underestimated."

What Are You Eating?

Food is another area where women first found their way into the workplace. As concerns about health and food safety have become more important, some women have made progress in helping people to eat better and feel safer about what's in their food.

Indra Nooyi, who was born in Chennai, India, in 1955, became chairman and CEO of PepsiCo in 2006. She had attended Madras Christian College in India and earned an MBA from Yale University. Most people think of PepsiCo as a company that makes Pepsi and other soft drinks, but Nooyi was determined to change Pepsi's reputation. As the US rate of obesity grew, she knew that there was a market for healthier drinks and snacks. She has pushed PepsiCo into producing more foods from vegetables, fruits, grains, and nuts. As the US population ages, there is also a greater demand for healthier products, and Nooyi hopes to increase PepsiCo's revenues with products for this market. She sees PepsiCo's products as falling into three categories: fun for you (regular chips, soda, and snacks), better for you (diet or low-calorie products), and good for you (foods such as oatmeal). Nooyi is also interested in the possibility of creating snacks that are aimed specifically at a certain age group, such as teens, pregnant women, or senior citizens. She says of her plans for the company's future, "I'm providing the same great taste ... so you don't have to make a choice between health and taste. We can bring the best of our normal products ... and make them affordable and available because of our scale, but then we bring you nutrition credentials as well."

Nooyi says that PepsiCo is no longer a soda company, and only 25 percent of its global revenue comes from carbonated drinks. Of PepsiCo's

Indra Nooyi, chairman and CEO of PepsiCo, has helped push the company into producing healthier food and drinks.

revenue, 25 percent now comes from water and noncarbonated drinks, which Nooyi feels will "future proof" the company. People all over the world are starting to think about what is really in their food and drinks, a trend that Nooyi is incorporating into the future of her company.

GMO FOODS

GMO foods began receiving a lot of negative attention in the late 2010s, but what exactly are they? GMOs, or genetically modified organisms, are living organisms, but with their genetic material artificially changed in a laboratory using genetic engineering. This creates combinations of plant, animal, bacteria, and virus genes that would never occur in nature. GMOs are usually created for a specific reason, such as to make plants that are resistant to herbicides or can produce an insecticide themselves. But they are also used to prevent things like brown spots in apples. Crops like corn, soy, canola, and sugar beets are most likely to be genetically modified. GMO crops are controversial because they may be linked to health problems, as well as causing damage to the environment, and violating the rights of farmers and consumers. These crops are common ingredients in packaged foods as well as in animal feed, which means that they become part of many animal products like eggs, meat, honey, and seafood. GMO crops are also producing superweeds and superbugs, which are resistant to standard herbicides and can be killed only with excessively toxic poisons. While some countries require any food product with GMO ingredients to state it on the label, the United States and Canada do not yet require GMO labeling.

Put It on the Label

Another woman who pushed her company toward healthier foods is Denise Morrison, CEO and president of Campbell Soup Company. She was born in New Jersey in 1954 and went to Boston College. Before becoming part of Campbell Soup in 2011, she worked for Kraft Foods, Nabisco, Nestlé, and PepsiCo. Campbell's Soup is one of the most familiar brands of processed foods in the United States but the brand has not been associated with "real food." Even artist Andy Warhol's famous painting of Campbell's soup cans underlined its place in American culture as a familiar processed, nonhomemade brand.

That changed when Morrison took over leadership of the company. She wanted to focus more on the company's foods and their place on family dining tables, instead of thinking of them as just products to be shipped all over the world. "Now as a company we're talking more about what's in our food and how it's made," Morrison says. "And we have a philosophy that our brand should be something we're proud to serve at our own tables." Part of this new approach was to remove artificial ingredients and colors from their foods. But the company went a step further and became the first major food company to label all ingredients that come from genetically modified organisms (GMOs) used in its products, such as corn, sugar beets, or soy. They even created a website called What's In My Food?, where consumers can go to easily find out what the ingredients in Campbell's

Denise Morrison, CEO and president of Campbell Soup, feels that leadership should include mentoring other women and giving back to the community.

products really are. They have also started Healthy Communities programs in several cities, as well as buying companies that produce fresh foods.

Morrison stresses the importance of leadership beyond just transforming Campbell's into a food company that operates on transparency with its products. "For me, leadership is service and there's power in giving and giving back . . . whether it is working in communities that are less fortunate or working with the next generation of women leaders to mentor them and make sure I'm sharing stories with them to help them be successful."

CHAPTER FOUR

RULING THE ONLINE WORLD

W omen also hold high-level jobs in businesses that are involved with the internet and how we use it for communication and interaction. Almost every popular social media tool has a woman—or many women—in executive or creative positions.

Perlman's Programming

Radia Perlman, who was born in Portsmouth, Virginia, in 1951, has the distinction of being called the mother of the internet. She is a software designer and network engineer, known for her invention of something called the Spanning Tree Protocol (STP). It might sound like something to do with nature, but it is actually an innovation that made today's internet possible.

Perlman was a student at the Massachusetts Institute of Technology (MIT) in the late 1960s and early 1970s and was one of only about fifty women out of a class of one thousand students. There were so few women that Perlman didn't even notice, until one day when she found herself in a class with another female student. She told Rebecca J. Rosen of *The Atlantic*, "I'd notice that it kind of looked weird … this other gender person looking curiously out of place in the crowd. I'd have to remind myself that I was also that 'other gender.'"

Perlman was working for the Digital Equipment Corporation in 1985 and trying to solve the problem of how to share files between computers. She invented the STP as a kind of traffic pattern for the internet to follow, with extra links if one link failed. It made it possible for the Ethernet to handle huge networks. Perlman also worked on ways to introduce children to programming and is working on ways to improve security on the internet.

Perlman doesn't care for her title "mother of the internet." She doesn't feel that there is only one type of person (such as kids who like to take things apart) who makes a good software engineer, male or female. "The kind of diversity that I think really matters isn't skin shade and body shape, but different ways of thinking."

Technology Out of the Way

Not all women working for internet companies are computer programmers or software engineers. Isabelle Olsson works as an industrial designer for Google. Olsson, who is Swedish, was born in 1983. She worked for a design company called Fuseproject when she was recruited by Google to work on their Google Glass project. Google Glass is a form of wearable technology, similar to a smartphone, but

Isabelle Olsson, senior industrial designer for Google Inc., speaks about the Google Home Mini voice speaker during a product launch event in San Francisco, California, on October 4, 2017.

worn as eyeglasses. It is hands free and operates through voice commands. Olsson explained her interest in working on a new design for the product after watching people on a bus, hunched over their phones: "Haven't we evolved to be human beings who can stand up straight and walk and use our hands and talk to people? And what if we can design something that lets us live in the moment and have technology be out of the way when [we] don't need it?"

The first designs were more about technology than appearance, and the glasses were clunky and unattractive. "When I first joined I had no idea what I was going to work on. Then I walked into a room full of engineers wearing a prototype of the glasses. These were very crude 3D-printed frames with a cellphone battery strapped to the legs. They weighed about 200 grams [about half a pound]." Olsson told the engineers to remove everything that wasn't absolutely essential and to hide what they could behind the frames of the glasses. The result has been styles of Google Glass that people won't be reluctant to use. Olsson will continue to refine the designs for Google Glass to better meet what consumers want ... and are willing to wear.

Seeing How the World Will Change

Susan Wojcicki is another executive who got her start at Google. She was the company's sixteenth person

Susan Wojcicki, CEO of YouTube, started her career in technology with the realization that technology was going to change the world.

hired, starting as their marketing manager in 1999. Wojcicki was born in California in 1968 and graduated from Harvard. She had planned on getting a PhD in economics and teaching. But then she discovered technology when she worked a summer job at a tech startup company. "[There are] moments where you see something but the world hasn't seen it yet, and you understand how the world is going to change in the future." She realized that technology was going to change the world and went back to Harvard and took computer science classes. She then went to work for a consulting company, earned a master's degree at UCLA, and worked for Intel before going to Google. One of her earliest jobs there was to create the Doodles that appear on the Google home page. As Wojcicki moved into bigger roles at Google, she realized that YouTube was competing with Google's video service, so she proposed that Google buy YouTube. It did in 2006, and in 2014 she became CEO of YouTube.

Wojcicki is determined that YouTube will continue not only to evolve, but will also build communities. "Our goal, really, is to take this amazing technology, continue to grow it, make it available to all people around the globe, across all platforms, and for all creators. It's a big mission."

"Speak Up, Believe in Yourselves, Take Risks"

Sheryl Sandberg is another tech executive who got her start at Google. She was born in Washington, DC,

WOMEN IN TECHNOLOGY

Susan Wojcicki is honest about the limitations and biases that women face when they work in the technology industry. During the summer of 2017, this was highlighted when a memo written by a male engineer at Google was leaked to the public. It said, in part: "At Google, we're regularly told that implicit (unconscious) and explicit biases are holding women back in tech and leadership. I'm simply stating that the distribution of preferences and abilities of men and women differ in part due to biological causes ... and that these differences may explain why we don't see equal representation of women in tech and leadership."

Wojcicki stated publicly that she has encountered bias in her industry, but Google has been an excellent place to work. When her daughter asked her "Mom, is it true that there are biological reasons why there are fewer women in tech and leadership?" she responded simply, "No, it's not true."

in 1969 and went to Harvard University. Sandberg worked for the World Bank and then for the US Department of the Treasury under President Bill Clinton. When the administration changed in 2000, Sandberg moved to California and began working for

Sheryl Sandberg, COO of Facebook, has started a foundation for women in business called Lean In.

Google. She liked Google's mission, "to make the world's information freely available" and spent seven years with the company as vice president of global online sales and operations.

Facebook founder Mark Zuckerberg recruited Sandberg in 2008 to work at Facebook because he wanted someone more experienced in management. Sandberg joined the company and helped to finally make it profitable. While she still works at Facebook, Sandberg has become best known for advocating for women in the business world, saying that they need to be more aggressive to succeed. In 2003, she published her book *Lean In: Women, Work, and the Will to Lead*. At the same time, she started an organization called Lean In, an education and community-building organization for women in business.

Sandberg continues to work and advocate for women. "We can each define ambition and progress for ourselves. The goal is to work toward a world where expectations are not set by the stereotypes that hold us back, but by our personal passion, talents and interests. Speak up, believe in yourselves, take risks."

Make Why Your Favorite Question

Marne Levine, who is the chief operating officer (COO) of Instagram, has a professional background similar to Sheryl Sandberg's. She attended Miami

Marne Levine, COO of Instagram, previously worked for the US Treasury Department and as vice president of public policy for Facebook.

University and Harvard Business School and also worked for the US Treasury Department from 1993 to 2000. She then spent four years working as vice president of public policy at Facebook, traveling constantly. "You name a part of the world, I traveled to it," she said. Facebook purchased the instant photo service Instagram in 2012, and Levine became the COO of Instagram in 2014.

OBSESSED WITH PHOTOS

Instagram was created by Kevin Systrom and Mike Krieger and launched in October 2010 as a free mobile app exclusively for the Apple operating system, but later for Android users as well. In 2012, it was sold to Facebook for $1 billion in cash and stock. Instagram owes its growing success to the fact that people are now obsessed with taking photos and posting them on social media. The popularity of smartphones, which can not only take photos, but also help users post them on social media instantly, has created a whole new market for photo-sharing apps. Instagram is specifically intended for sharing photos and videos taken by smartphones. Instagram users have a profile and a newsfeed, similar to those on Facebook and Twitter. When users post a photo, it is also displayed on their friends' newsfeeds. Basically,

(continued on the next page)

(continued from the previous page)

Instagram is a simplified version of Facebook, emphasizing mobile devices and visual sharing. While users can view Instagram on their computers, they can only upload photos using a mobile device. Instagram also has a Stories feature, where users can see the story or stories added to photos and posted by their friends over the last twenty-four hours or create their own stories.

In her two years as COO, Levine has expanded Instagram with locations in eight countries and doubled its number of users. She feels that some of Instagram's success is because of the women who use it. "Women are drawn to Instagram because it's a storytelling platform, and women have always been incredible storytellers," she says. But she also travels around the world and meets with female entrepreneurs, encouraging them especially in countries where it is difficult for women to make their way in business. She has also contributed to Sandberg's Lean In organization and is also a director of Women for Women International. Her best advice for women is, "Make 'Why?' your favorite question. It feeds your curiosity."

Optimistic About the Future

As the head of trust and safety at Twitter, Del Harvey has to deal with the darker side of social media. Born in 1982, Harvey is very secretive about her past and won't even say if she graduated from college. She does admit that she has had an unusual career path before working for Twitter. She was a pool lifeguard at a state mental health institution, gave psychological tests to contestants on TV reality shows, and pretended to be a child for an organization called Perverted Justice, in order to capture online sexual predators. In 2008, when the online messaging service Twitter began to have trouble with spam, she became their twenty-fifth employee.

Harvey's job has evolved as Twitter has grown, with more than three hundred million users. She was once the only employee in her department, but now she is one of many people who deal not only with spam, but also with abusive behavior and user safety as well as harassment, pornography, and even terrorism. They also have to balance their precautions with freedom of speech and with cultural definitions of what really is inappropriate. "A lot of people are surprised I'm not super pessimistic," Harvey says. "But the negative interactions are significantly outweighed by the positive ones. And that makes me optimistic about the future."

Twitter values free expression, but with a half billion tweets taking place every day, Harvey's job is to make sure that Twitter doesn't become a place where negative speech and interactions scare away users and advertisers. "Your one-in-a-million chance of something going horribly wrong happens 500 times a day," says Harvey. "My job is predicting and designing for catastrophes." When Twitter tried to replace users' abilities to block unwelcome people from following and retweeting their posts with a "mute" feature that simply hid the posts, Harvey herself warned that

Twitter is one of the most popular online news and social media services on the internet. Del Harvey tries to uphold free speech rights while blocking what is truly inappropriate.

it would make cyberbullying easier. And Twitter users were so outraged at the change that Twitter changed its mind in just twelve hours and returned the blocking option. As the internet and social media become an increasingly important part of how people interact with each other, people like Del Harvey will have to keep adapting to new threats as well as new opportunities.

CHAPTER FIVE

ENABLING ENTERTAINMENT

Women have also made great progress in the entertainment industry. They have moved into executive roles at networks and media companies, design video games, and have become nationally and internationally known journalists.

On the Air in China

Yang Lan is a Chinese media entrepreneur, journalist, and talk show host. She was born in Beijing in 1968 and earned a college degree in English language and literature. She entered the job market at a time when Chinese women were still supposed to be pretty, pleasant faces reading scripts on television. Yang Lan had done some acting in college and decided to audition for the first-ever national open audition for a position

Yang Lan, often called the Oprah Winfrey of China, hosts two popular television talk shows in China as well as running Sun Media Group.

on Chinese television. She was competing with a thousand other young women for a role as the moderator on the new *Zheng Da Variety Show*. Yang said,

> The producer told us they were looking for some sweet, innocent and beautiful fresh face. So when it was my turn, I stood up and said, "Why [do] women's personalities on television always have to be beautiful, sweet, innocent and, you know, supportive? Why can't they have their own ideas and their own voice?" I thought I kind of offended them. But actually, they were impressed by my words.

Yang Lan was given the role and ended up on the first Chinese television show that allowed the hosts to speak freely instead of reading from a script. She had around two hundred to three hundred million viewers. She left the show after four years to take graduate courses in film and journalism in the United States.

Yang Lan returned to China, and in 1998, she launched her own television talk show, called *Yang Lan Studio*. It was intended to be the kind of in-depth talk show developed by American journalists such as Barbara Walters. In 2000, she and her husband created Sun Media Group, which includes television production, newspapers and magazines, and online publishing. They launched Sun TV, which would be China's first cultural and historical channel. Yang Lan changed the name of her interview program to *Yang Lan One on One* and expanded it to include even more international issues, such as the economy, culture, and politics. She later launched a television show called *Her Village*, aimed at urban Chinese women and intended to empower them. In 2005, Yang Lan also founded the Sun Culture Foundation. As one of China's wealthiest women, she wanted to encourage other wealthy Chinese to become active philanthropists. The foundation supports poverty relief, education, and understanding between countries and cultures. The foundation has partnered with Peking University, Columbia University, and Harvard University to offer educational development for civil and nonprofit organizations.

Yang Lan's career reflects the changes in China itself. Her grandmother was part of a generation in which many women had bound feet, and few girls ever learned to read. Her mother was the first woman in her family to attend college. Yang Lan herself never watched television as a child. Her career has focused on improving women's place in Chinese society, as well as urging China to use its new wealth to help its people. "To be a more respected country in this world, we should show our moral dignity instead of just our spending power."

LAND OF BILLIONAIRES

China is second only to the United States in the number of billionaires, with two hundred people whose personal wealth is more than $1.5 billion. This compares to about four hundred billionaires in the

Zhou Qunfei, a former factory worker, founded Lens Technology, which makes glass screens for iPhones. She is also the wealthiest self-made woman in the world.

(continued on the next page)

(continued from the previous page)

United States. China is also the home of more than half of the world's wealthy, self-made women, with eleven of the top twenty richest female entrepreneurs. In fact, the world's youngest self-made billionaire is Chinese. Zhou Qunfei, age forty-seven, is the founder and CEO of Lens Technology, which makes glass screens for iPhones. Her net worth is estimated to be more than $9 billion, which would also make her the richest self-made woman in the world. China's female billionaires are "the product of the Chinese Communist party's commitment to gender equality, which [allowed] women to flourish after capitalism started to take hold," says Huang Yasheng, an MIT professor and expert on China's entrepreneurs. Philanthropy is also growing in China as a result of so much wealth, and many rich families are starting their own charitable foundations.

"Fearlessness Is Like a Muscle"

Arianna Huffington has made her name as a syndicated columnist, an author, a radio host, and a businesswoman. She became famous for the Huffington Post, a Pulitzer Prize–winning online newspaper that she founded and served as editor-

Arianna Huffington, founder of the Pulitzer Prize—winning Huffington Post, now dedicates herself to working with individuals and companies to promote health and well-being.

in-chief of until its sale to AOL in 2011 and her departure in 2016. Huffington was born in Greece in 1950 and lived in England before moving to the United States in 1980.

Once in the United States, Huffington worked as a conservative political commentator, appearing on television, but gradually her political viewpoint became more liberal. She has also written several books, two biographies, and an exploration of Greek myths. In 1986, she married Michael Huffington who worked for the US Department of Defense and later was elected to be a member of the US House of Representatives. In 2003, she ran for governor of California against Arnold Schwarzenegger but lost. After writing a *New York Times*–bestselling book about corporations and greed, she started the Huffington Post in 2005. It was a website that included a blog, liberal viewpoints, and news, and eventually began covering other areas of news, such as sports and business. The site won a 2012 Pulitzer Prize for national reporting.

Huffington left the Huffington Post in 2016 to start Thrive Global, a new digital platform that would be dedicated to health and wellness. When she suffered an injury after fainting from exhaustion and overwork, she decided to dedicate her energies to helping people and corporations find a balance between work, good health, and enjoying life. She continues to write books that are intended to help people succeed and overcome their fears.

Fearlessness is like a muscle ... the more I exercise it the more natural it becomes to not let my fears run me. The first time we take that first fearless step, we begin to change our lives. And the more we act on our dreams and our desires, the more fearless we become and the easier it is the next time. ... [W]e can definitely get to the point where our fears do not stop us from daring to think new thoughts, try new things, take risks, fail, start again, and be happy.

The Most Powerful Woman in Television

Bonnie Hammer is another woman who has succeeded in what seemed to be a man's world of broadcast media and telecommunication. With more than 128 million Americans watching shows on the cable channels she oversees, she is called the most powerful woman in television. She is chairman of NBC Universal Cable Entertainment Group, which includes ten television networks (including USA Network, E!, Bravo, and SyFy) and two cable television studios.

Hammer, who was born in New York in 1950, attended Boston University and earned degrees in communications and media technology. She started her television career at the public television station WGBH in Boston, producing shows like *This Old House* and *Zoom* before moving on to network television.

She worked as an original programming executive for the Lifetime network before joining Universal Television in 1989 as a programming executive. In 2004, NBC merged with Universal and Hammer became president of several networks and later chairman of NBC Universal. She works to create individual "voices" for each network, to help them stand out in a competitive industry. She is also working to make several of the cable channels she runs less gender specific, so that there aren't women's networks and men's networks, which limits viewership.

Hammer has received awards for both her work and her social activism. She created a campaign called Erase the Hate, as well as a public service program called Characters Unite that was meant to address hate and discrimination and promote tolerance. Characters Unite now includes public service

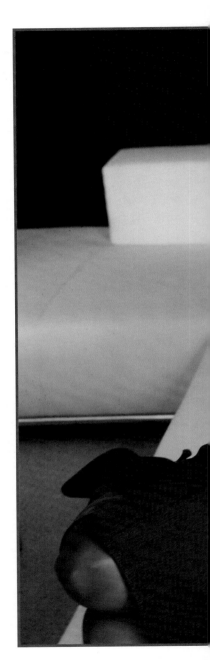

Bonnie Hammer is the chairman of NBC Universal Cable Entertainment Group and is often called the most powerful woman in television.

announcements, themed
episodes of shows in cable
channels, a website, and high
school and community outreach.

At the age of sixty-five,
Hammer feels that she is still
relevant and valuable and
has no plans to retire. She
told the graduating class of
2017 at Boston University that
"Television, at its core, is a
platform for telling stories. ...
[And] the reason we started
telling stories in the first place
[is that] they help us understand
things we didn't before."

Stuck on the Corporate Ladder

Even women who have achieved
high positions in industries like
telecommunications may find
that they get stuck as they climb
the corporate ladder. An example
of this is Marni Walden, who
as executive vice president is
Verizon's highest-ranking female
executive and the only woman to
report directly to the Verizon CEO. In October 2017,

Marni Walden, executive vice president of Verizon Communications Inc., spoke during the TechCrunch Disrupt San Francisco 2016 Summit.

she announced that she would be leaving Verizon in early 2018. "There was one other job at Verizon [that of CEO] and it became clear that job potentially wasn't going to be mine," Walden said.

Walden started at Verizon in 2014. She entered the telecommunications industry almost by accident, when her first job after graduating from California State University was selling briefcase phones, which were large, heavy, early versions of cellphones that had a two-hour battery life and were really only useful in cars. Once she was hired by Verizon, she worked her way up from president of Verizon's Midwest region to Verizon Wireless's vice president and chief marketing officer and then president of product and new business innovations. She finally reached the position of executive vice president and president of global media, and it was assumed that she'd be next in line for the position of CEO. In her time at Verizon, she helped it purchase AOL in 2015 and Yahoo! in 2016.

Walden has stated that she is disappointed in how few female executives there are at Verizon, despite efforts to improve gender balance at the company. She notes that fostering more women in a company requires starting with low and midlevel jobs and also having the support of male executives to sponsor women in higher positions. But she also advises employees who feel stuck on the corporate ladder not to be afraid to take a risk at times. "You don't always have to stay for the security of what you know," she said. "Stepping out and being bold is scary at times, but it's also incredibly fun."

WHO'S BETTER?

The computer programming industry is still dominated by men, with roughly 73 percent of programmers being male. But studies also show that women are often better programmers. A study was conducted based on data from GitHub, an open-source software community with more than twelve million users who collaborate on coding projects by suggesting solutions to various problems. A member can suggest a solution to a coding problem and GitHub will accept it if it is a useful and valid solution. Researchers thought that women would have fewer acceptances, but it turns out that they have a higher rate of acceptance than men, and in every computer programming language. However, when the programmers were identified as women in their profiles, then the percentage of their acceptances dropped.

Not Your Average American Woman

One industry where women have had to fight hard to make their way is in the video-game industry. Women haven't traditionally been viewed as being good at computers and technology, especially women who were born in the fifties and sixties. And Carol Shaw, who was born in 1955 and was designing video games in their early years, admits that she was not an average American woman. She grew up around science and technology and knew that she was good at math, so she ignored the gender barriers that would usually keep women out of these kinds of careers. Shaw studied computer programming at college, earning degrees in electrical engineering and computer science from the University of California, Berkeley. After college, Shaw got a job with Atari, programming games for its gaming console. Shaw said she chose Atari because "I got paid to play games." Even though she was the only female video-game programmer at the time, she was used to being the only woman in her computer science courses, so it didn't bother her. She became one of the world's first professional video-game designers.

Video games at that time were entirely created by one designer, including the graphics, sound, and programming, from start to finish. Shaw's first game was a 3D version of tic-tac-toe. Even though games at that time had a limited amount of memory to use, Shaw became so good at creating a kind of artificial intelligence within her games that other programmers around the world would study her work. She did a version of checkers and other games for Atari. She later worked for another gaming company, Activision, and created a scrolling shooter game called *River Raid*. The game was a huge hit and received many awards. Shaw also created a game called *Happy Trails* and did some other projects for Activision, but then the video-gaming industry became less

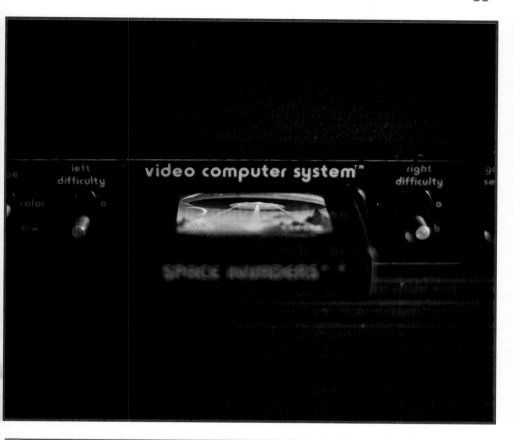

left difficulty   video computer system™   right difficulty

color

b w

SPACE INVADERS

Carol Shaw worked at Atari after college. The Atari Video Computer system, which played games such as *Space Invaders*, was once the cutting edge of home gaming consoles.

profitable. She went to work as a computer language programmer and was so successful that she was able to retire in 1990.

Shaw's success in an industry dominated by men was mostly because of the fact that she refused to believe what people told her were appropriate things for girls to do. "When I was in junior high and high school, I was good at math. I entered a bunch of math contests and won awards. Of course, people would say, 'Gee, you're good at math—for a girl.' That was kind of annoying. Why shouldn't girls be good at math?" Since retiring, Shaw has volunteered for Foresight Institute, an organization focused on future technologies and the transformations they will bring.

1875 Lydia Pinkham begins marketing her herbal remedy for women.

1919 Sarah Breedlove (Madam C. J. Walker), America's first female self-made millionaire, dies.

1920 Congress establishes the US Department of Labor Women's Bureau to represent wage-earning women and promote legislation for them.

1941 A huge campaign by government and industry is launched to persuade women to take jobs during World War II.

1942 Actress Hedy Lamarr coinvents a radio frequency device used to encrypt messages.

1950 The number of businesses owned by women reaches one million.

1960–1979 More women start businesses, partly because the increased divorce rate makes single women seek higher-paying jobs.

1963 The Equal Pay Act of 1963 passes, requiring that men and women receive equal pay for equal work within the same company.

1985 Radia Perlman invents the Spanning Tree Protocol, which helps make the internet possible.

1988 Congress passes the Women's Business Ownership Act to end financial discrimination against women-owned businesses.

2000 Martha Stewart becomes America's first self-made female billionaire.

2000–2013 Many business and financial institutions create programs to financially support women entrepreneurs.

2002 Gwynne Shotwell joins Space X and eventually becomes president.

2005 Arianna Huffington starts the Huffington Post.

2012 Ginny Rometty becomes the first female CEO of IBM.

2013 Mary Barra becomes CEO of General Motors, the first woman to hold that position among the Big Three Automakers.

2014 Oprah Winfrey becomes America's first female African American billionaire.

GLOSSARY

administrative Having to do with running a business or organization.

artificial intelligence The ability of a machine or computer to imitate intelligent human behavior.

artistry A creative skill or ability.

beautician A person whose job is to style hair or perform beauty treatments.

bias Prejudice in favor of or against one thing compared to another thing.

colleague A coworker or teammate, especially in business.

credential A qualification or achievement that shows someone's abilities.

dictate To give orders or tell someone exactly what to do.

discrimination Unfair treatment of people based on categories like gender, race, or age.

entrepreneur Someone who starts or operates a business, usually with some financial risk.

favela A Brazilian shack, slum, or shanty town.

frequency The rate at which vibrations occur in a radio wave.

GMO A genetically modified organism, which has been changed by humans to result in a specific feature.

innovative Featuring new ideas or methods, original and creative.

managerial Having the function, responsibility, or position of a manager or leader.

mentor An experienced and trusted advisor or teacher.

pamphlet A small booklet with information about a single subject.

patent The exclusive right, granted by a government, to make, use, or sell something for a certain amount of time.

platform A computer's operating system and the software it will run.

protocol A special set of rules used in telecommunication connections.

revenue The income or earnings of a company or organization.

software The programs and operating information used by a computer to perform tasks.

syndicated Relating to material that is published or broadcast in multiple newspapers or on television stations at the same time.

transparency The quality, in a business or government, of being honest and open.

underprivileged Not having the same rights or standard of living as most other people in a society.

FOR MORE INFORMATION

American Business Women's Association (ABWA)
9820 Metcalf Avenue, Suite 110
Overland Park, KS 66212 USA
(800) 228-0007
Website: http://www.abwa.org/pages/home-page
Facebook: @ABWA.NationalOrganization
Twitter: @ABWAHQ
The American Business Women's Association's
    mission is to bring together businesswomen and
    provide opportunities for them to grow personally
    and professionally.

Canadian Association for Women in Business
    Network
703 Bloor Street West (201)
Toronto, ON M6G 1L5
Canada
(416) 993-2083
Website: http://www.womeninbiznetwork.com
Instagram and Twitter: @thriveincanada
The Canadian Association of Women in Business
    Network is community of collaborative, fun,
    supportive, influential, and ambitious women
    business owners who aspire to achieve a life filled
    with passion, purpose, and profit.

Canadian Business Chicks
6619 Silver Springs Crescent NW
Calgary, Alberta T3B 3Z2
Canada
(403) 606-8869
Website: https://canadianbusinesschicks.com
Facebook and Twitter: @cdnbizchicks
Canadian Business Chicks is Canada's first inclusive
women's networking community. It provides
women at every stage of life and career with a
safe environment to connect, learn, share, mentor,
collaborate, and inspire.

National Association of Professional Women (NAPW)
1325 Franklin Avenue #160
Garden City, NY 11530
(866) 540-NAPW (6279)
Facebook: @NAPWhq
Instagram: @napwinc
Twitter: @NAPWInc
Website: https://www.napw.com
The American Business Women's Association
provides professional networking, career services,
educational opportunities, and networking events
for professional women.

National Association of Women Business Owners
(NAWBO)
601 Pennsylvania Avenue NW
South Building, Suite 900
Washington, DC 20004

(800) 556-2926
Website: https://www.nawbo.org
Facebook: @NAWBO
Twitter: @NAWBONational
NAWBO represents more than ten million women-owned
businesses in the United States, in economic, social,
and political spheres of power worldwide.

National Center for Women & Information Technology
(NCWIT)
University of Colorado
Campus Box 417 UCB
Boulder, CO 80309
(303) 735-6671
Website: www.ncwit.org
Facebook: @ncwit
Twitter: @NCWIT
The American Business Women's Association is
the only national nonprofit focused on women's
participation in computing, helping nearly nine
hundred organizations recruit, retain, and advance
women from K–12 and higher education through
industry and entrepreneurial careers by providing
support and action.

Women in Technology (WIT)
200 Little Falls Street, Suite 205
Falls Church, VA 22046
(703) 349-1044
Website: http://www.womenintechnology.org
Facebook: @WITWomenDC

Twitter: @WITWomen

WIT is dedicated to advancing women in technology, from the classroom level to the executive level. They offer leadership development, technology education, and networking and mentoring opportunities for women at all levels of their careers.

FOR FURTHER READING

Bryant, Jill. *Phenomenal Female Entrepreneurs* (Women's Hall of Fame Series). Toronto, ON: Second Story Press, 2013.

Diehn, Andi. *Technology: Cool Women Who Code* (Girls in Science). White River Junction, VT: Nomad Press, 2015.

DiPiazza, Domenica. *Space Engineer and Scientist Margaret Hamilton* (Stem Trailblazer Bios). New York, NY: Lerner, 2017.

Ignotofsky, Rachel. *Women in Science: 50 Fearless Pioneers Who Changed the World*. New York, NY: Ten Speed Press, 2016.

Lasky, Kathryn. *Vision of Beauty: Candlewick Biographies: The Story of Sarah Breedlove Walker*. New York, NY: Candlewick Press, 2012.

Lewis, Anna. *Women of Steel and Stone: 22 Inspirational Architects, Engineers, and Landscape Designers* (Women of Action). Chicago, IL: Chicago Review Press, 2014.

May, Vicki V. *Engineering: Cool Women Who Design* (Girls in Science). White River Junction, VT: Nomad Press, 2016.

McCully, Emily Arnold. *Ida M. Tarbell: The Woman Who Challenged Big Business—and Won!* New York, NY: Clarion Books, 2014.

Robbins, Dean. *Margaret and the Moon*. New York, NY: Knopf Books for Young Readers, 2017.

Schatz, Kate. *Rad Women Worldwide: Artists and Athletes, Pirates and Punks, and Other Revolutionaries Who Shaped History*. New York, NY: Ten Speed Press, 2016.

Shen, Ann. *Bad Girls Throughout History: 100 Remarkable Women Who Changed the World*. New York, NY: Chronicle Books, 2016.

Tougas, Shelley. *Girls Rule! Amazing Tales of Female Leaders* (Girls Rock!). Minneapolis, MN: Capstone Press, 2013.

BIBLIOGRAPHY

Biography.com. "Arianna Huffington: Journalist (1950–)." Retrieved October 16, 2017. https://www.biography .com/people/arianna-huffington-21216537.

Biography.com. "Hedy Lamarr. Retrieved October 12, 2017. https://www.biography.com/people/hedy -lamarr-9542252.

Biography.com. "Madam C. J. Walker: Entrepreneur, Civil Rights Activist, Philanthropist (1867–1919)." Biography.com, April 27, 2017. https://www .biography.com/people/madam-cj -walker-9522174.

Biography.com. "Sheryl Sandberg: Business Leader (1969–)." Retrieved October 14, 2017. https:// www.biography.com/people/sheryl-sandberg.

Blaszczyk, Regina. "Women in Business: A Historical Perspective." Smithsonian Institution. Retrieved October 16, 2017. http://amhistory.si.edu /archives/wib-tour/historical.pdf.

Bort, Julie. "IBM CEO Ginni Rometty told this inspiring story about her husband." Business Insider, June 20, 2015. http://www.businessinsider.com/ibm -ceo-ginni-rometty-tells-inspiring-story-about-her -husband-2015-6.

Catalyst. "Quick Take: Women in the Labour Force in India." Catalyst, June 27, 2017. http://www .catalyst.org/knowledge/women-labour-force-india.

Davidson, Martha. "Innovative Lives: Janese Swanson, Beyond Pink and Fluffy." Smithsonian National Museum of American History, March 3,

2005. http://invention.si.edu/innovative-lives
-janese-swanson-beyond-pink-and-fluffy.

Edwards, Benj. "VC&G Interview: Carol Shaw, Atari's
First Female Video Game Developer." Vintage
Computing & Gaming, October 12, 2011.
http://www.vintagecomputing.com/index.php
/archives/800/vcg-interview-carol-shaw-female
-video-game-pioneer-2.

Forbes. "*Forbes* Profile: Bonnie Hammer." Retrieved
October 16, 2017. https://www.forbes.com
/profile/bonnie-hammer.

Harvard University Open Collections Program. "Lydia
Estes Pinkham (1819–1883)." Women Working,
1800–1930. Retrieved October 13, 2017. http://
ocp.hul.harvard.edu/ww/pinkham.html.

Holmes, Mark. "It All Started with a Suit: The Story
Behind Shotwell's Rise to SpaceX." Satellite, April
21, 2014. http://www.satellitetoday.com
/publications/2014/04/21/it-all-started-with-a
-suit-the-story-behind-shotwells-rise-to-spacex.

Home Depot. "Ann-Marie Campbell, Executive Vice
President—U.S. Stores." Home Depot Leadership.
Retrieved October 13, 2017. https://corporate
.homedepot.com/leadership/ann-marie-campbell.

Horowitz, Julia. "Former Xerox CEO Ursula Burns:
Government needs to help lift up the poor." CNN
Money, July 25, 2017. http://money.cnn
.com/2017/07/18/news/ursula-burns-american
-opportunity/index.html.

Laden, Tanja M. "Maj Isabelle Olsson, Lead Industrial
Designer of Google Glass, on Wearable

Technology." Flavorwire, June 28, 2013. http://
flavorwire.com/401024/googleglass.

Pearson, Samantha. "Maria das Graças Foster,
Petrobras chief." *Financial Times*, January 30,
2015. https://www.ft.com/content/64b0703a
-a703-11e4-8a71-00144feab7de?mhq5j=e5.

Powell, Anita. "Find the Beauty in African Sales." *New
York Times*, November 15, 2012. http://www.
nytimes.com/2012/11/16/fashion/16iht
-fbeauty16.html.

Raczek, Weronica. "Retail's 8 Most Powerful Women."
RIS, September 9, 2016.   https://risnews.com
/retails-8-most-powerful-women.

Rosen, Rebecca J. "Radia Perlman: Don't Call Me
the Mother of the Internet." *The Atlantic*, March 3,
2014. https://www.theatlantic.com/technology
/archive/2014/03/radia-perlman-dont-call-me-the
-mother-of-the-internet/284146.

Seabrook, John. "Snacks for a Fat Planet." *New Yorker*,
May 16, 2011. https://www.newyorker.com
/magazine/2011/05/16/snacks-for-a-fat-planet.

Vinton, Kate. "YouTube CEO Susan Wojcicki On
Confidence, Women In Tech And Why She
Convinced Google To Buy YouTube." *Forbes*, May
31, 2017. https://www.forbes.com/sites
/katevinton/2017/05/31/youtube-ceo-susan
-wojcicki-on-confidence-women-in-tech-and-why-she
-convinced-google-to-buy-youtube/#25cbc81d40a1.

Yang Lan. "The Generation that's Remaking China."
TED Talk, October 3, 2011. https://www.ted.com
/talks/yang_lan/transcript.

INDEX

About the Author

Marcia Amidon Lüsted has written multiple books and magazine articles for young readers. She also writes business profiles and has met and interviewed many women entrepreneurs. You can learn more about her books at www.adventuresinnonfiction.com.

Photo Credits

Cover Jerod Harris/Getty Images; p. 7 Leland Bobbe /The Image Bank/Getty Images; p. 11 Michael Ochs Archives/Getty Images; pp. 16, 18, 32, 34–35, 56, 63, 65, 68, 88–89 Bloomberg/Getty Images; p. 21 Alex Wong/Getty Images; pp. 24–25 Timothy A. Clary/AFP /Getty Images; p. 28 Eric Carpenter/Moviepix /Getty Images; pp. 38–39 © AP Images; p. 42 Jim Spellman/WireImage/Getty Images; p. 45 Hulton Archive /Archive Photos/Getty Images; p. 47 Jay Paull/Archive Photos/Getty Images; pp. 50–51 Paul Morigi /Getty Images; pp. 52–53 © Ringo Chiu via ZUMA Wire; p. 59 Emma McIntyre/Getty Images; p. 70 Scott J. Ferrell/CQ Roll Call Group/Getty Images; pp. 74–75 Anadolu Agency/Getty Images; p. 78 Chip Somodevilla /Getty Images; p. 81 STR/AFP/Getty Images; p. 83 Angela Weiss/AFP/Getty Images; pp. 86–87 Carolyn Cole/Los Angeles Times/Getty Images; p. 93 Robee Shepherd/Moment/Getty Images; cover and interior pages (gold) R-studio/Shutterstock.com.

Design and Layout: Nicole Russo-Duca; Editor and Photo Researcher: Heather Moore Niver